Healthy Food, Healthy Dog

Affordable Ways to Improve Your Dog's Health Through Food

Jennifer Davis

Mare's Tales Publishing, LLC

Healthy Food, Healthy Dog by Jennifer Davis
Published by Mare's Tales Publishing, LLC

© Copyright 2018 Mare's Tales Publishing, LLC. Printed and bound in the United States of America. All Rights Reserved. No part of this book may be reproduced in any form or by any electronic or mechanical means, including information storage and retrieval systems, without written permission from the publisher.

Publishers Cataloging In Publication
Healthy Food, Healthy Dog/Jennifer Davis.
p. ; cm.

ISBN: 978-1981618293

Dedication

To the mighty Warrior Princess, my dearest Bella, who has joyfully and confidently placed her health into my hands. No matter what tomorrow brings, we have had a good run, my dear. You have been such a gracious teacher. Thank you for being in my life.

Acknowledgements

Many people have helped us on this unexpected journey, and we are thankful for each and every one. Margaret Stewart and Melinda Harvey guided my first uncertain steps toward the world of holistic veterinary medicine. They sat with me, cried with me, let me talk endlessly about Bella without interruption, and cheered us on, despite their own heartbreaking losses during that time. Jean Locke, who came to me through the mysteries of social networking, helped me share Bella's story far and wide. Rosemary Louden provided me with a magical, inspiring space to begin writing this book.

We are also grateful to Bella's veterinary team: Dr. Jacoba Nassar, who first discovered Bella's cancer and who has literally had her hands on Bella every month since then to ensure her little lymph nodes remain discrete to the touch; Dr. Jacqueline Ruskin, who introduced us to holistic practices and canine nutritional options; and Dr. Carrie DeRegis and Dr. Debbie O'Keefe, Bella's oncologists who must be the most patient women in the world, given my constant questions. We assembled a great team of medical caretakers who were endlessly supportive and kind. I'm so grateful for that support and for the telephone calls during which they encouraged me and, at times, honestly disagreed with me. The gift they gave me was to allow me to make my own choices without judgment. I am grateful for their skilled care, unwavering kindness, respect, and, most of all, love for Bella.

The SCAT (Southern Connecticut Agility Team) agility club, where Bella and I run agility, has been amazing in its support of Bella and her health. Every run is celebrated, and the warmth I experience from this group is so special. Additionally, I appreciate the occasional smacks upside my head when I focus too much on performance and not as much on the gift of being present.

My family is endlessly patient with me. With the exception of my sister, I do not come from a pet-loving family, so I cannot imagine what they must be thinking as I talk about Bella at every family gathering. Nevertheless, they support and encourage me, occasionally even patting Bella if she's around.

Bella and I have met countless guardians dealing with their dog's cancer on this journey of ours. Truly, it feels like canine cancer has reached an epidemic level. To all of you who follow us on social media, who reach out to us with your questions and comments and statements of support, we wrote this book for you and for those who come after you. If we can help one family do a little better, then we have accomplished our goal. We send you all love.

And we wish to acknowledge those who have passed from lymphoma during our journey. So many dogs. So many, many dogs. Each has become a new star in the sky, leaving behind broken hearts. Appearing to us in our dreams, our beloved and departed pets encourage us to do better, to be more thoughtful, and to share more information. We love you. We feel you walking beside us. We miss you all.

Table of Contents

Introduction 9

Our Story 13

The Canine Immune System 25

Probiotics and Digestion 31

How to Read a Bag of Kibble 35

Raw vs. Home-Cooked: Which is Better? 43

How Much to Feed? 49

YOU Are the Most Important Ingredient of All 55

Recipes 59

Resources 69

About the Author 71

Introduction

Many books and articles about canine nutrition are heavy on science and short on common sense. The topic isn't usually considered light reading for a Sunday afternoon, but that is my goal for this book. There is so much information available now – books, online articles, and scientific treatises – that it's easy to become overwhelmed. With this book, I intend to distill information from a variety of trusted resources into an easily digestible format, so you can make good decisions for your pet without becoming mired in confusion and frustration.

It's interesting to think about why people would pick up a book on canine nutrition. Generally, people seek additional diet information when their dog is having a health crisis. Most likely it's a cancer diagnosis, a long-time battle with a skin allergy, or a lifetime digestion issue. Whatever it is, at some point many people come to the realization that they can do better when it comes to feeding their dogs.

Canine nutrition became a focal point in my life through just such a crisis. I am not scientifically trained. I'm not a veterinarian. I'm not a canine nutritionist. I am a layperson who has had dogs all her life. I've fed them good quality kibble, and I've managed fluctuations in their health without a lot of thought until a cancer diagnosis for my corgi brought me up short. As I entered the world of canine cancer care, I was completely out of my depth. Our lives began to revolve around check-ups, lab tests, and chemo appointments. I felt helpless, and I turned to food for my dog as a way of participating in her care and showing her my love and support. I was like a mother making chicken soup for her sick child because I literally didn't know how else to deal with her diagnosis. I knew nothing about food then. I know a little more now.

When I started outlining this book, the first thing I wrote down was, "What would I like to see? Five years ago, what did I want to know?" What you will see here, then, is a reflection of what my needs were when I first started to live with Bella's cancer diagnosis. I wanted to know more about the immune system; I wanted to know how to understand the differences between kibble and home-cooking and raw; and I wanted some recipes. In short, I wanted to know where to start.

The second thing I wrote down was, "Who is this book for?" Some of you may follow Bella's Facebook and Instagram accounts where I've shared some of our recipes. We received many requests for a book, so for those of you who have asked, here it is. It is my hope that these recipe ideas will travel far and wide, so other families seeking to shift their dog's diet will find them, use them, and have the courage to create their own.

My goal for this book is to provide you with the tools you need to feed your dog in ways that you can afford and manage. I have distilled information here from a variety of trusted sources into an easily readable format, so you can make good decisions for your dog without becoming mired in confusion and frustration.

The first tool is knowledge. I'll talk about the immune system, so you can understand how that system works and how you can impact it in negative or positive ways. I'll also talk a little bit about the canine digestive system and how it's a crucial player in overall immune functioning.

The second tool this book will hand you is courage. I intend to give you the courage to go out and try things that might work for your dog's issues. The pet food industry makes this all sound so complicated and overwhelming, leading us to believe we can't do this. But we can, and many of us do. So can you.

The final tool is creativity, based on a combination of the first two tools. The recipes I've given you are basic – you can spin them off in your own direction to utilize what is locally sourced, seasonally available, and within your budget and time constraints.

This booklet is not meant to be a definitive study on canine digestive health, nor is it meant to be the only answer to your pet's health crisis. Rather, it is a starting point for tweaking your dog's diet and a springboard to help you to dive further into canine nutrition research, as there are scores of good resources available including dynamic canine nutritionists to guide you online and in person.

My hope is that while you will most likely read this book in one sitting, the knowledge you take away with you will last for a lifetime of pet companionship.

Our Story

Until December of 2012, canine cancer was an unnoticed speck on my horizon. My dogs all lived to be 15, 16, and even 17 years old, and never had I needed to care about cancer. My agility club has an annual cancer fundraiser, but, quite frankly, I always paid little attention to the message and just enjoyed the games.

This all changed for me on December 22, 2012. At the time, my Pembroke Welsh corgi, Bella, was a mere five years old. My dear companion and I played agility together and slept in bed together. I fed her kibble, walked her, bathed her, and took her to the vet regularly for checkups and shots – all the things you're supposed to do to take care of your dog.

One day, I noticed the lymph nodes under Bella's jaw were swollen. I assumed she had a cold and made an appointment with her vet for the following week. At the appointment, I remember my vet sitting on the floor, checking all Bella's lymph nodes, and explaining how dogs have more than just the two I knew about. She was telling me they could be swollen because of this or that. Or, because of cancer. I joked, "Just tell me she isn't going to die."

She was healthy, right? And only five years old. My dogs don't die at five years old. The look the vet gave me took my breath away, but I managed to tamp down the fear while she aspirated Bella's lymph nodes before we went home.

The vet called the next day to confirm the diagnosis of lymphoma and schedule an appointment for Bella with the oncologist before the upcoming holiday. At the oncologist, I was told all Bella's lymph nodes were involved. Her spleen was enlarged. Because of this, she was probably at Stage 4. There are only 5 stages.

I'm not sure how much of this information I actually heard at the time. It was only when the oncologist suggested Bella start her chemo treatment *that day* that I began to comprehend the magnitude of the situation. Bella and I were entering a whole new challenging world together, a world full of fear, anger, tears, new friends, knowledge, and hope.

On the advice of good friends, I also took Bella to a holistic veterinarian. I wanted to do everything I could to support her through the chemo. I was fortunate to find a holistic vet who provided us with supplements that would support and rebuild Bella's immune system during, as well as after, the chemo. She also recommended I start Bella on a raw diet. I went home with a bag of supplements and six pounds of commercial raw food. It was a start.

For 16 weeks (plus three or four "off" weeks), I transported Bella to the oncologist's office for treatment. Bella would receive Vincristine, a chemotherapy medication, on the first and third weeks of each round, which had a debilitating effect. She would go from lively and dancing to depressed and weak, only to rise up at the end of the week and take another dose. Even in those early days, I found myself trapped between the oncologist and the holistic vet, with one insisting the holistic supplements diminished the efficacy of the chemo and the other countering that the supplements were necessary for Bella to survive the chemo. I learned to be my Bella's advocate relying only on my gut because, truthfully, that's all I had at the time; I didn't know anything.

Between rounds two and three and after round four, Bella stayed for three days at the holistic vet's office to receive an intravenous Vitamin C treatment to flush the toxins and chemo by-products from her liver. I didn't really understand why I was doing that, and it was very expensive, but the idea of flushing the liver and kidneys of chemo by-products and dead cancer cells appealed to me. Cleaning her system and readying it for more work made sense to me. I didn't know the science behind it, but I understood the common sense of it. As an aside, during this process, we discovered Bella only had one kidney!

- I meticulously collected all Bella's medical records and lab tests, carrying them around in a large notebook to every appointment, pouring over them at night, and trying to understand what they meant for my dog. I read magazine articles, books, and internet blogs about canine cancer, cancer treatments, and foods. I joined lymphoma support groups and canine nutrition social media pages, trying to find answers.

In May of 2013 Bella was deemed "in remission." The oncologist handed her back to me and assured me there were other drugs we could use when she came out of remission in September.

"In September."

It sounded like it was pre-scheduled. After crying on my good friend Melinda's shoulder about the unfairness of it all, and the expense, and how I couldn't go through this again, I resolved to continue doing everything in my power to keep that from happening. From my readings, I understood that we couldn't go back to our past practices of kibble, vaccinations, topical pest controls, and environmental stressors. We had to continue with the healthy changes we had made to support Bella during chemotherapy in order to have a chance of keeping her in remission.

For a long time, Bella and I were successful in holding back the cancer. We achieved an agility title, and we learned a new sport – canine scent work. We lived our lives. I believed if I just tried hard enough and did everything right, Bella and I could make cancer go away. Although by now I had learned the population of dogs who never came out of remission was minuscule, I was sure Bella would be in that group. I even started to use the language of "cured."

Bella stayed in remission for 53 months, coming out in June of 2017. She has since regained her remission after two rounds of chemo and, at this writing, is lying here by my feet while I write. Throughout this ordeal, I have often wondered, "Why? Why have Bella and I been successful where many others have not?" After years of soul-searching, I believe I've found the answer: every day, Bella and I work together to support her wellness and good health. We don't fight cancer – we support good health. That's all we can do.

Since diagnosis, I've tweaked my dog food routine in a number of ways because this isn't just about Bella. In 2012, my nine-year-old collie, Taegan, was diagnosed with chronic IBS and skin allergies. In 2015, we were joined by Fern, a Scotch collie puppy with the dietary needs of a developing young body. Finally, in 2016 came Winston, a rescued corgi who was apathetic and drastically underweight because of facial nerve damage preventing him from closing his mouth.

BELLA

17 | Healthy Food, Healthy Dog

TAEGAN

FERN

WINSTON

These four dogs have been my school. They have taught me more about canine nutrition than I could have imagined. They have graciously accepted (most) of my experiments, and they have grown strong and healthy with my foods. At 10 years of age, Bella is lean and energetic, still competing in agility and in remission from cancer. Fern has grown into a glossy, sleek athlete at two years old. Winston has gained four pounds. He has a gleaming red coat, a boundless zest for life, and, happily, his appallingly bad breath from his constantly opened mouth is gone. Taegan lived to be 14. During his last few years, the diet I implemented for him eliminated his IBS episodes, cleared up his skin, and eradicated the doggy smell from the house that had clung to him for years.

The Right Food for Your Unique Dog

This is all about food and about feeding your dog *the way she needs to be fed*. Take note: your dog has her own needs, and not all dogs should be fed the same way. My four have slightly different meals. Does preparing them take a little time? Of course. About 15 minutes twice a day. Bella gets special supplements measured and added in. Winston needs his food mushed to a particular texture, which requires a ground kibble product. Fern requires extra calories because she is never still, so I add an egg, sardines, or some fat to her meal. Taegan received certain oils to address his skin and coat as well as additional probiotics to support his gut health.

Truth be told, while I credit Bella's diagnosis with my "awakening," Taegan had a host of issues that were my first warnings something was very wrong in my home. In early 2012, he was afflicted with a horrible case of mange. We shaved him from head to toe and gave him a weekly bath of some really rough chemicals for four weeks to kill the mange. During the months he was naked, I had to dress him in socks and a T-shirt to keep him from biting and scratching himself raw. On top of the mange, the vet diagnosed him with a low-functioning thyroid requiring lifetime daily medication. He was medicated, and I was frustrated. I couldn't seem to help him, and I was beginning to resent the time and expense of taking him to the vet.

I know now that Taegan's afflictions were signs of a terribly impaired immune system and poorly functioning microbiome (community of microbes), but I didn't know that then. It wasn't until we changed our routines at home when Bella was diagnosed that Taegan received additional food and support from me. I understand now that he wasn't receiving the nutrition he needed to heal and repair.

Taegan had been on his new diet about four years when, at the age of 13, he had his first and only episode of bloat. When he was X-rayed, the vet brought me in to look at his films. "Look at this," she said, "This dog is amazing. Except for this gas, there's nothing here. All his organs are perfect. He is a perfectly healthy dog."

My 13-year-old dog's insides looked like those of a much younger dog. The lesson here is that health comes from the inside. That's what food does. Food is so powerful it can help an animal come back from poor health into good health. As for Taegan, he went on to live another year-and-a-half after his bloat episode.

Much of what I've read over the past few years confirms that what we feed our dogs is critical to the successful treatment of some cancers and other systemic diseases. But how wonderful would it be to start before there's a diagnosis, so maybe there will never be a diagnosis at all?

A NOTE ABOUT CANCERS

There are many types of cancers. As I understand it, lymphoma is the cancer most responsive to chemo. My experience is limited to lymphoma and chemo, so that's what we'll talk about here. Your dog may not have the same diagnosis or may not be receiving chemo, but the theories behind immune support are all the same. Rebuild the immune system. Strengthen it. Don't impose upon it. Let the immune system do its job.

As guardians of our dogs' health, we must be advocates. As such, we are called upon daily to make choices from an overwhelming array of options about our dogs' nutritional needs, healthcare, and vaccinations. We are surrounded by advertising for foods, topical pest treatments, and medications, so even though we aren't trained scientists or nutritionists, we need to be educated consumers to make these sophisticated choices for our pets. We must understand the choices – what they are and what they are not. These decisions are reachable for us. The act of feeding our dogs well isn't beyond our skills. We feed ourselves; we feed our children. We can feed our dogs. Increasing our knowledge can bolster our faith in our ability to make the right choices for our dogs, which we can and will do because no one knows our dogs as well as we do.

Think of it this way: even improving two or three meals a week is better than nothing. Everyone is busy, has finite funds, and carries many responsibilities. Improvements here or there are just that – improvements. My hope for you is that you take on what you can handle and what you can afford, building on that as you can. Give yourself time to learn. Give yourself the opportunity to experiment. Be encouraged by the changes you make, and don't judge yourself negatively because you aren't doing more.

As the majority of readers are here because of a cancer diagnosis or systemic disease, that's where we'll start. Now, stop thinking about what you could have or should have done differently. Let's redirect that good energy and move forward to addressing immune system health every day.

The Canine Immune System

When you enter the world of canine cancer – and this really holds true for any diagnosis of a systemic illness — a lot of scientific terms get tossed about, and it's easy to get confused. You may look at your dog's lab results and wonder, "Is this good or is this bad?" This basic primer on the canine immune system will help you understand how it works, what might be happening with your dog, and what you can do to support your dog with food, so you can better understand those results. Certainly, there are many articles online and some books you can read that will go into detail about the research and the science, and I encourage you to dig deeper as you wish. My focus here is to talk about the immune system as it relates specifically to canine lymphoma, but this information can be applied to allergy and GI tract issues as well.

To begin, picture the immune system as a multi-part structure. The first major part of this system you see every day – the skin. The skin covering the body protects the interior from foreign substances. It is supported in its role as the primary immune defender by stomach acid, the mucus of the respiratory system, and the gastrointestinal tract (GIT). We'll talk more about the GIT in the chapter on probiotics. The first step in determining your pet's health, then, is to check the skin. Is it clean and flake-free? Is it intact or are there small cuts, wounds or insect bite marks that make it vulnerable? Are there parasites like fleas and ticks present? Does your dog have a pleasant smell, or are you conscious of a "doggy odor" when you walk into the house? Is the coat dry and scratchy and brittle or soft and supple and glowing? Does your hand come away greasy after stroking your pet? Is your dog itchy, or does she chew her feet? These are things you can look for every day that will give you a read on the overall health of your dog. Some of the first signs of trouble we see will be in the skin and coat.

The digestive system is the next building block of the immune system, which we will also discuss in greater detail in the chapter on probiotics. For the purposes of this chapter, it suffices to say that it's a major player in the immune system, and when it's completed its job, cells move out of the digestive system into the body, which is where we're headed next.

The part of the immune system deep inside the dog that picks up when digested nutrients move into the cells of the body is known as the adaptive system. This gets a little technical, so hang on. The adaptive cells are designed to thwart specific invaders like bacteria, viruses, and cancer cells. They "remember" invader cells, so they can react faster and stronger when they encounter them again. This is known as the "immune response."

The cells of the adaptive system are known as phagocyte cells, of which there are three major types: monocytes and macrophages, granulocytes, and lymphocytes. If you look at your dog's lab results, you may see those words. These cells are designed to "read" a foreign invader that has stimulated them with an antigen (an antigen is any substance which produces an immune response). The phagocyte cells produce an antibody, which is a protein that interacts with an antigen, stopping the foreign cell in its tracks. The phagocyte cell will attach to the antigen with the antibody, destroy the foreign cell, and then "remember" it within the system, so the body can continue to successfully attack and destroy that invader.

The information about the invader cell is passed between phagocytes by cells that are called cytokines. There are even cells called antigen-presenting cells, which engulf antigens and process them into a form that can be recognized by lymphocytes, which then destroy the modified antigen. The immune system does this all day, every day, for the life of the body.

There are two types of lymphocytes: the B-cell and the T-cell. A diagnosis of lymphoma is often referred to as either B-cell or T-cell, which is really too bad because it implies that these cells are bad, and they're not. In fact, my vet once told me "B" is for "bad" and "T" is "terrible," but I think this short-hand does us a real disservice, and we need to understand how these lymphocytes work.

Basically, you want B-cells and T-cells in the body. Both these cells are created in the bone marrow, so we want a healthy bone marrow. The immature cells then migrate, with T-cells going to the thymus gland where they mature and B-cells either staying in the bone marrow or going to the liver, which is where they mature.

The canine thymus gland is located in the front chest cavity between the trachea and the ribs. This gland grows rapidly through puberty and then slows down. The T-cells there mature into one of two types: the mighty killer T-cell (also known as the cytotoxic T-cell), which seeks out and destroys cancer cells, or a helper cell that assists other lymphocytes in mounting a strong immune defense.

Meanwhile, the liver and bone marrow are producing mature B-cells that move through the bloodstream, destroying foreign invaders in their way. These cells tend to accumulate in the lymph nodes and spleen which is why, when the system goes into overdrive, your dog may have enlarged lymph nodes or an enlarged spleen. Bella had both at the time of her first diagnosis.

As you can see, B-cells and T-cells are necessary for a successful immune system, as long as they are operating properly. The cancer related to these cells stems from not producing enough, producing too many, or a die-off, so the diagnosis refers to a malfunction in the system itself.

Two other players you will see in your lab results are eosinophils and neutrophils. These cells are also our friends. Eosinophils are white blood cells. They ingest bacteria and other foreign cells and help destroy cancer cells. Neutrophils are scavenger cells. They ingest and destroy antigens and cell debris and are an important step in detoxing the cellular environment. When you look at your dog's lab results, you want to see numbers within the normal range here.

So, what happens to create disease in our dogs? Well, many times the lymphocytes meet a foreign cell, create an antibody to defeat the antigen, and the thing is done. But disease, in its most simplistic terms, is an insufficient immune response. Sometimes it's called immunodeficiency or suppression. The cells begin to operate abnormally. The phagocytes are unable to produce the necessary antibodies to attack the antigen, and the antigen-presenting cells are unable to engulf the antigens and create a readable form for the phagocytes. Cancer and systemic disease come from a malfunction of an intricate, balanced system due to the introduction of something that the immune system can't recognize or deal with. This system works beautifully – until it doesn't.

You can see, then, the importance of having a strong, vibrant, well-functioning immune system to address foreign viruses and bacteria. Our goal is to limit the types of foreign invader cells our dogs' immune systems get exposed to over time. By introducing heavy metals and manmade chemical cells, we are exposing the immune system to invaders outside the scope of its knowledge. Simply put, the body is unable to create the appropriate immune response. It can't "read" the invader, which means it can't stop the invader.

As we increase the amount of man-made toxins in our dogs' environment, we increase the number of challengers the immune system has to figure out how to address. We expose our dogs to vaccines, topical pest controls, dryer sheets, scented candles and plug-in infusers, lawn chemicals, heavy metals, road salt, cleaning products, perfumes, and aftershave every single day. These products introduce foreign invaders to the immune system, which is set up to fight off bacteria and viruses but not petrochemical cells. The immune system does what it can but, at some point, becomes overwhelmed with fighting off human-made cells. While one of these products on its own may not cause cancer or a massive allergic reaction, taken together, day after day for years, it creates a scenario the immune system cannot handle.

When Bella was diagnosed, I had my pumpkin spice candle burning in winter and my mango candle ablaze in summer. I had my dryer sheets. I fertilized my lawn four times a year and used an aromatic product that made my floors shiny and looking new. All day, every day, Bella and Taegan were inhaling these chemicals and absorbing them through their feet.

We can make changes. Now, my house has no scented products, and it smells great. It's an old New England house with a natural woody smell. Not doggy, not chemical. My floors and counters are scrubbed with vinegar, water, and a few drops of peppermint essential oil, and they are clean and sanitary. My clothes are washed with scent-free detergent, and I use these cool, felted woolen balls in my dryer to keep my clothes fluffy and static-free. My yard is not a manicured golf course, but it's full of bugs for the chickens, green growth for my viewing pleasure, and lots of rabbits and birds. It's a fine yard, and, most important, it's safe for my dogs.

I use natural products for pest control. I spread diatomaceous earth under my trees. I place homemade tick tubes into my wood pile and stone walls where the dogs can't get them. I flea-comb my dogs to remove any ticks they pick up on our walks. I have to brush my dogs anyway, so why not make it part of our pest control regimen? I have natural cedar and lemongrass products I spray on their legs and tummies when we're walking in the woods. I vacuum the floor and cushions regularly and wash their bedding as flea control. This is all do-able. We have had one flea this year. I know that because I caught it in a flea comb, and Bella immediately stopped scratching. This is not about destroying the pest population; this is about controlling it.

We can make these kinds of changes judiciously. Reducing exposure to toxins and petrochemical products means better health for everyone in the family, not just your dog. Because I no longer use scented products, I can smell someone's use on the far side of a room now; these things are potent. When I step outside and inhale someone else's dryer sheet, I can literally feel those oily cells clinging to my nostril hairs. This reminds me of how resoundingly toxic these products are. To not use them is an easy, affordable, and pain-free choice you can make to support your dog's immune system.

Probiotics and Digestion

No book about canine nutrition would be complete without a discussion of the canine digestive system. So much is written about this system, but, again, my focus is to give you an overview, so you can build your own meals to meet your dog's needs.

Good health begins with good gut health, a discussion that really isn't as overwhelming as you might think. The digestive tract is a hugely important player in the immune system as it is populated with healthy bacteria, which break down food into nutrients that can be absorbed by the intestinal tract and into the body.

The digestive system primarily includes the stomach and the small and large intestines. It also has "accessory" organs, which include the salivary glands, pancreas, liver, and spleen. Its function is <u>digestion</u> of food, <u>absorption</u> of nutrients into the body (which are produced from the broken-down food), and <u>prevention</u> of toxic substances from entering the body. Cells along the digestive system release hormones that trigger enzymes to be discharged from the pancreas and liver. These trigger cells help the system work fluidly. At the end of the process, the digestive system produces waste including undigested materials, expelled toxins, and bacteria. That's what you gather in your poop bags, which is pretty remarkable when you think about it.

With that as our very simplistic digestive system background, we can now say that the intestinal walls are lined with a tremendous amount of lymph tissue, which creates lymph cells. This tissue includes the mucosal lining, the microbiome with probiotics, and antigens. This is where the beneficial gut bugs live, which is why this system is so important to the immune system. A healthily functioning system will move nutrients through the appropriate pathways and into the body while pushing toxins out of the body and out of the dog. It regulates itself as well as the substances seeking to pass through it. As my locksmith says, "Good guys in, bad guys out."

What happens when this system isn't working as it should? You've probably heard the phrase "leaky gut," and if you're anything like me, the visual wasn't pretty. What that term means is that the digestive system isn't functioning the way it needs to, and the tightness of the cells that keep the toxins from being absorbed by the body has loosened allowing toxins and other non-nutrients to break through the lining, move into the body cells themselves, and take up valuable room from the nutrients. It's like having a pile of boxes in the room, so there's no space for your furniture. What this looks like in your dog shows up as a number of symptoms and diseases: arthritic joints, diabetes, cancer, weight gain, thyroid disease, skin allergies and dermatitis, low energy, irritable bowel flare-ups, etc. Remember, if a healthy gut makes a healthy dog, the converse is also true: an unhealthy gut makes an unhealthy dog.

There are innumerable reasons why your dog might have poor gut health. A systemic infection can wipe out a gut colony, as can our treatment of those infections. Anti-inflammatory steroids are devastating to a microbiome in that they can cause suppression of the immune system, which opens the door for opportunistic secondary infections. A round of antibiotics is also destructive because an antibiotic doesn't discriminate between the bacteria causing the illness and the good little bacteria further on down the digestive line doing their job to enhance digestion. Both bacteria will be killed by the antibiotic.

Please note I am not saying that you shouldn't use these drugs for your dog. They are often a necessary part of keeping our pets healthy. I am saying, however, that there are repercussions from that use, and you can and should address those repercussions biologically, so your pet can heal and be well again. In his first year with me, Winston suffered from a number of infections – bladder infections to upper respiratory infections to pneumonia to an optic nerve inflammation – and antibiotics and steroids were a key part of our recovery strategy, particularly to help him regain his sight. However, just like with Bella and her cancer, I added specific foods to his diet to enhance his recovery and his health, so these infections and their treatments did not overwhelm his system.

There are two other significant culprits leading to a leaky gut that are easy to fix and very much within our control. First is poor nutrition. If your kibble has excessive grains, it will create yeast bacteria in the gut during the digestive process, which eventually overwhelms the gut bacteria. When the gut bacteria cannot break down the food appropriately, the gut loses its ability to discriminate between nutrients and toxins, and it lets the toxins pass deep into the dog's cells causing leaky gut. This is where you start to see a dog become stiff-jointed, overweight, and lethargic.

Second is toxic overload. By living with us, our pets are exposed to toxins every day through their digestive system and their skin. Herbicides and pesticides used on our lawns and streets stick to pads and are then ingested through licking. When our dogs lie on the lawn in the sun, they're soaking up the chemicals used to kill weeds through their skin. Our indoor floor-washing products are constantly on their feet and tongues. The emissions from the candles we burn are in their lungs. Excessive vaccinations, topical pest treatments, monthly de-worming products – all of these impact the immune system and the gut. And for those of us dealing with cancer, chemo contributes a toxic overload to a delicately balanced system.

The good news is that we can handle this by providing good nutrition, cleaning up our environment, and getting probiotics into our pets. If you buy a commercial probiotic product, you'll want to make sure that it contains a good array of bacteria including acidophilus and bifidus. Yoghurt contains probiotics and is safe for dogs, but to get as much as your pet needs, a powdered or herbal probiotic is a better choice. To provide a friendly environment to receive the probiotics into your dog's gut, she should first eat prebiotics. These are found in the fiber of fruits and vegetables, but don't go crazy – a little bit, finely minced or lightly steamed to start to break down the cellular structure, goes a long way.

One of the best ways to introduce probiotics to your dog is through fermented products. A fermented food is created by a process called lacto-fermentation, where a naturally occurring bacteria feeds on the sugar and starch in the food, creating lactic acid. This acid preserves the food and creates beneficial enzymes, b-vitamins, Omega-3 fatty acids and a plethora of probiotics.

You can buy these products or you can make your own. Other excellent sources of fermentation are kefir and kombucha. If you use a purchased product, first make sure that it does not contain onions. We'll talk more about prohibited foods in a later chapter, but if you pick up a great product from the shelf and it has onions – just put it back. I tend to use a lot of fermented cabbage for my pack, which I either dice finely and add to food or toss into the blender when making veggie mix. You'll see more of that in the recipes section.

If your dog needs to be on antibiotics, anti-inflammatory steroids, or chemo, up the probiotics she's getting. Winston has been on a long course of antibiotics to treat a resistant UTI infection as well as a steroid to deal with temporary sight loss. Along with his regular probiotic, I give him some raw goat's milk from a trusted, clean source and extra fermented ginger and sauerkraut. Your vet should be able to guide you on probiotic dosages. Make sure that's part of your support for your dog.

How to Read a Bag of Kibble

I am not wholesale anti-kibble. While it is not my choice for a primary protein source, I do understand that for many people there are not a lot of affordable options. However, you can enhance your kibble choice. I feed some kibble - my Winston requires ground-up kibble so that he can get the necessary texture for eating, and I've chosen one for him that is grain-free, high in calories for weight gain, and free of synthetic vitamins. I want you to choose your kibble well, use it wisely, and store it properly.

To start to understand the world of kibble and how to read the bag so you really know what you're getting, first you must understand the related regulatory environment. This morass of information is what makes feeding our dogs feel so complex, but broken down into its parts, it's not so hard.

There are a lot of players in the regulation of pet food production. The Food and Drug Administration (FDA) and the United States Department of Agriculture (USDA) are the federal agencies in charge of safe production, interstate sales, labeling, and food branding, but neither agency reviews nor controls kibble recipes. Instead, the Association of American Feed Control Officials (AAFCO) partners with the FDA to publish animal feed guidelines and to define ingredients. The standards they have developed are voluntary in the industry, and AAFCO has no enforcement authority. Additionally, it doesn't do any independent analytical testing of dog foods. Rather, it relies upon studies performed by pet food manufacturers.

Two things you need to know are that no agency has the job of independently analyzing and confirming recipes, and no agency has the authority to enforce recipe regulations. We're on the honor system here.

There are probably a half-dozen other state, national, and international regulatory agencies that impact our feeds here in the U.S., and there's a whole body of literature on problems within the industry that I won't get into here. You can do your own research and come to your own conclusions.

There are many articles and videos online showing you how kibble is made. At its most basic level, the ingredients are weighed, dried, blended into a powder, moistened, extruded into a shape, baked to reduce the water content, cooled, spun in a bin while fats and flavoring are sprayed upon them, stored until bagging, bagged, and, finally, shipped to a retailer. These bags of kibble have a shelf life of about 12-to-16 months. They're a strong contrast to raw and home-cooked food in terms of content and freshness! I would encourage you to find a video of the production of kibble to familiarize yourself with the process of extrusion.

Higher quality kibble is going to have pretty good packaging with grease barriers, so it's best to keep the kibble in the bag, out of the sun, and sealed tightly. When you buy kibble, you'll often see the bag is vacuum-packed. That prevents oxidation of fats by removing all the air inside the bag. As soon as you open the bag, however, oxygen gets in, and oxidation begins.

When fats oxidize, they are broken down into smaller compounds, which, over time, can damage the cell structures of the kibble protein. This can affect the chemical composition of your feed. As moisture gets into the bag, mold and bacteria can be produced, which can impact a dog's kidneys or liver over time. Keeping the kibble sealed tightly in its bag after opening slows this process. Also, while it's more expensive to buy small bags of kibble, they're a better choice if you don't feed it exclusively and only use a little at a time.

While researching this book, I came across a website with a question about maggots in the kibble, and was it still good to feed? The answer came back that it probably wouldn't hurt the dog but best to throw it out. We can be smarter than this. We shouldn't have to ask if "maggots in the bag" is a bad thing. It means the bag has been stored improperly (because flies got in), the fats are oxidizing, the proteins are breaking down, and the chemical composition of the feed is deteriorating. Clearly, this was a missed teaching moment on that website. We as consumers need to educate ourselves. If you use kibble, store your bags well.

Kibble bags (and cereal bags and snack bags, for that matter) smell good to dogs, even if there's no food inside. When a dog sticks her head into a bag, the interior Mylar-like freshness coating creates a vacuum-like seal around the dog's neck as she licks and breathes into the bag, causing it to tighten and cut off oxygen. The inability to breathe causes the dog to panic, and she will die a horrible death if the bag is not quickly removed. It doesn't matter how smart or strong your dog may be, these vacuum seals are powerful and fatal. There is an entire Facebook page dedicated to educating pet owners about pet suffocation, and you need to be aware of this risk. Store any bag like this out of reach, and cut them up prior to discarding.

Kibble Labeling

Pet food manufacturers add antioxidant materials to help maintain freshness. You may see one or more of these ingredients on the label: BHA, BHT, Ethoxyquin, or TBHQ. These are commonly added to the kibble mix to extend shelf life and stop the oxidation of fats once the bag is opened.

If you see these listed in the ingredients section of your kibble bag, I again encourage you to do your own research as you consider what your dog is being exposed to. These are human-made chemicals, not ones that naturally occur. Ethoxyquin is a pesticide – it's actually used also to stop a bacterial infection on pears, which means it kills living things (bacteria). Of course, we know that the gut has useful, necessary bacteria, so we have to question if we want a bacteria-killing ingredient in our feed. The USDA has confirmed in studies that ethoxyquin impacts liver enzymes, and the Center for Veterinary Medicine has asked the pet food industry for a voluntary limit of 75 ppm (parts per million). There are no long-term studies on the impact of lifetime exposure to ethoxyquin for canines. For me, it's a question of common sense. Since I know that a bacteria-killing agent cannot differentiate between "bad" bacteria and useful gut bacteria, I don't want to let that agent loose in my dogs' food.

BHA and BHT are classified as "endocrine interrupters," which means they can lower the production of certain hormones. Both have been linked to cancer in lab rats, particularly in the thyroid, but there are no canine studies published. Additionally, while the FDA deems BHA "generally recognized as safe" (GRAS), the National Institutes of Health (NIH) says it's "reasonably anticipated to be a human carcinogen." My take on this is to let the FDA and NIH fight it out; I'll look for a product that doesn't include BHA and BHT.

TBHQ, which is derived from butane, has been linked to pre-cancerous cells in the stomach linings of lab rats. There have been no long-term studies here, either, but it's butane, people! Again, not something I want to be feeding my dogs, any more than I want my dogs chewing on a butane lighter.

I tell you this not to panic you, but to encourage you to start to sort through your kibble ingredients. A better alternative might be Vitamin E, both synthetic and non-synthetic. Vitamin E is a successful antioxidant, but it is not as stable at the high cooking temperatures used to dry out many kibbles with high initial water content. Also used are rosemary extract, citric or sorbic acid, and calcium propionate. While these have their own issues in terms of synthesis and production, they are an improvement over man-made chemicals.

Lastly, look for cranberries, blueberries, and apples, which also are successfully incorporated into kibbles as antioxidants. These are more benevolent, less destructive antioxidant sources. The trade-off for you is time; when you move away from pesticides, chemicals, and synthetics into more natural preservatives, the product doesn't last as long. A good rule of thumb is the more natural the preservative, the shorter the shelf life of the kibble. Which brings us back to the smaller bags of kibble.

Under AAFCO standards, a pet food manufacturer has up to six months to reprint a label to indicate a change in the recipe. If your dog becomes ill right after you've opened a new bag, this may be the reason. I had successfully maintained my Taegan's IBS for years on high-grade kibble. Then, one day after I'd opened a new bag, his diarrhea came back with a vengeance. At the same time, Bella started to nibble around the edges of her food. The store I purchased from called the company, who assured us the recipe wasn't changed, so I assumed it was a bad bag. I picked up a replacement bag and had the same result, so I switched foods. Two months later, with much fanfare, the company announced its recipe was "new and improved" under new management.

Pay attention to "best by" dates and understand what they do – and do not – tell you. Dog food manufacturers are not required to post the actual date of manufacture of the food you are buying, so you can't really know how old your kibble is. Depending on its preservatives and packaging, your kibble choice could have been made weeks, months, or even a year earlier. Reread the earlier description of the extrusion process. Canned foods can be between two and five years old. What you do know is that as of the "best by" date, the quality will start to go down because that's really what that date means. It's not like we're aging a fine wine, and it will be the best on that date. The quality will start to go down fast right around that given date, so you're not getting a bargain if your retailer is trying to unload foods right around the "best by" dates.

Many people move to grain-free kibble upon realizing that ingredients like corn, rice, and wheat are just fillers. When looking at a bag of kibble, the first thing you have to know is that meat listed as the first ingredient signifies that by the pre-processing weight, meat weighed the heaviest of all the ingredients. The pet food manufacturer isn't required to tell you how much meat there is by the post-processing weight. In fact, they aren't required to give you any actual weight at all or to provide you with actual amounts of any ingredient. I guess it's proprietary, a trade secret. Nor are they required to include water in the list of weighed ingredients (obviously, whether used for processing or sucked out of the protein, water is the heaviest ingredient). The sole requirement is to list ingredients, heaviest to lightest, by pre-processing weight, exclusive of water content.

Cracking the Nutrition Panel Code

AAFCO has a large guide of about 170 pages addressing labels and display panels that pet food manufacturers follow in describing their products. Pet food manufacturers have to follow the guide in describing their products. It's pretty daunting to try to work your way through it. It's like a code, but we can crack it.

In order to say a product is 100% of a certain protein, it actually has to be 100% of that ingredient. There can be no other ingredients except water, and there could actually be more water than protein, depending upon the product. That's the easy one.

Some products claim they are 95% protein, which means that the protein derived from animal sources must by 95% of the total weight *before processing* (exclusive of water used). Of course, once it is processed into dry kibble form and the water is removed from the protein, it weighs less. Ultimately, it will make up much less of the total product weight, but if it started out as 95% before processing, then 95% it is.

The next group is the 25% cluster, which you'll see coupled with the words "entrée," "dinner," or "recipe." Just like in our example above, we start with 25% of total weight before processing and end up with much less after processing. What does it mean when it says "25% lamb and rice"? That's a tricky one. Under AAFCO rules, one of these must be at least 3% of the total product, and the other can make up 22% of the balance. Since proteins are the most expensive ingredient, it's not hard to do the math here.

A food is considered "complete and balanced" if it meets the proper amount of nutrients determined by AAFCO for all life stages – puppies, pregnant females, active adults, and the elderly. Somehow, this one food will meet all the dietary requirements of all of those different life stages? Common sense tells us this cannot be true, but it looks good on a label, and by providing consumers with one-stop shopping, it reduces manufacturing costs and facilitates buying choices for uneducated consumers.

Ingredients that are "natural" are from a plant, an animal, or the earth (via mining), and they can be either processed or unprocessed. The addition of synthetic vitamins and minerals is also acceptable under this label. "Organic" foods are any foods that meet the handling and production requirements of the USDA's definition of organic.

My guess is that as you move more into home-cooking, you'll find it surprisingly affordable, and you'll use less kibble. It's like deciding we don't want to feed our children fast food or prepared meals all the time, but allowing it to be a small part of their diet. Kibble may have its place for our dogs, but it doesn't have to be at the head of the table.

Raw vs. Home-Cooked: Which is Better?

With conversations about raw vs. home-cooked food for dogs, for every two people there seem to be three opinions. Many people who feed a raw diet are devoted to it and feed nothing else. Home cooks swear that nothing is better than what you make with your hands. People who feed kibble feel defensive and judged. Where does commercial raw fit it? Can you incorporate kibble into your plan? What if you don't have the time to home-cook or the money to feed raw?

What I would love to have you pull from this section is that you can improve what you are feeding to your dog, even if you're not ready to completely convert to a raw diet or home-cooked food. Study these approaches, and take from them what works best for you.

A raw diet, at its simplest level, is uncooked food. The attraction of the diet for many is the belief that you are feeding your dog as Mother Nature intended. However, there is more to it than slapping a pound of hamburger meat into your dog's bowl and calling it a meal. A raw protein has to be balanced with muscle, bone, and organ. It has to be varied. And then it has to include a good mix of fiber, fruit, and vegetable matter to provide the necessary vitamins, minerals, and amino acids into the dog's GIT. When in the wild, canids eat the entire animal; they don't simply eat the thigh meat. When we provide a raw meal, we obviously aren't going to make sure that hair or feathers are included, but we do need to be aware that there is more to nutrition than what is found in the muscle meat or breast.

Guardians committed to a raw diet carefully source their proteins and often have a freezer designated for storing them. They may raise their own poultry or rabbits for their dogs, and they may obtain a side of beef or a deer carcass to be broken down and stored. The proteins will be weighed out and ground together in an 80-10-10 ratio: 80% muscle meat, 10% ground bone, and 10% organ. Finally, the guardian will add the veggies, fruits, and oils they feel are sufficient for their dog's appropriate nutrition. Many vets object to a raw diet because of concerns about the completeness of nutrition, which you need to be aware of if shifting to a raw-based diet. Be prepared for your vet to cringe when you announce you are feeding raw, and have on hand your list of supplements and add-ons that meet your pet's nutritional requirements, so you can have a productive conversation about nutrition.

Commercially prepared raw diets can help you meet your dog's nutritional requirements because they incorporate not only the proper ratio of muscle, bone, and organ but also vegetables, fruits, minerals, and other nutrients. Some commercial providers have developed a freeze-dried kind of raw, but it's more common to see raw food prepared with high pressure processing (HPP) after packaging. HPP is a cold pasteurization technique that doesn't actually cook the proteins. This cold-processing method is used not only for raw diets for pets but also for many foods consumed by humans. HPP is intended to extend shelf life and kill micro-organisms. However, since it doesn't use heat, the nutritional integrity of the raw protein remains undisturbed. As the level of pathogenic infiltration is substantially lessened by HPP, concerns that a micro-organism in the food may be transmitted to the dog and then the household are alleviated. Many vets raise concern about salmonella, which isn't a problem for dogs (look at all the icky stuff they love to eat without issue) but is a problem for us, so, of course, we want to minimize that risk. We never experienced a problem during the many years Bella ate a commercial raw food before we switched to our present resource.

When reviewing the ingredients list of a raw food product, you should see varied proteins (necks, organs, maybe fish, etc.) plus fruits and vegetables, perhaps kelp or seaweed, seeds, and natural preservatives. Unlike the ingredients list for a bag of kibble, you may find that you recognize most, if not all, of the ingredients. Freeze-dried raw can be a great food to start with on your journey toward raw as well as for traveling when you want the health benefits of raw and the convenience of kibble. Again, it's all about reaching an appropriate balance for you and your dog.

Feeding raw does require you to handle meat at some point. Many vets express concern about contamination from this, but most of us handle meat for our families in our kitchens already. You wipe down the counters after every meal, and you scour the sink after every thawing. These are common-sense solutions. You shouldn't refrain from feeding raw simply because you're afraid you might forget to wipe down a countertop. If you buy a commercial raw product or you have a trusted source, you shouldn't have to worry about contamination in your home as long as you clean up after yourself.

Expense is another factor cited against raw. The short answer is yes, kibble products are a lot less expensive to buy than commercial raw products. The long-range answer, however, is less clear. Bella has been on a raw diet for five years, and during that time, she has experienced no need for veterinary care since her chemo was completed. She had no disease, no skin issues, and no dental problems. I feel comfortable saying I saved considerably on her vet bills. Fern has been a raw-fed dog her whole life, and she has incurred no vet bills for illness, disease, or dental care. Winston is another story; he's been raw-fed for less than a year and has struggled with frequent infections. However, his immune system was slammed by multiple vaccinations, and who knows what he was exposed to in the first two years of his life. Taegan experienced no issues requiring veterinary care in four years except for that single bloat incident.

My experience leads me to believe that over time, all three of my dogs will experience less disease. Certainly, they are healthy to look at and healthy to the touch, their teeth are clear of tartar, and they are pest-free and energetic. Again, balance is the key. If you want to try a raw diet for your dog, do it incrementally – start with raw on the weekends, or raw for one meal a day, or some raw with some kibble. All of these are sustainable options. Like I said at the beginning of this book, any change toward an improved diet is better than nothing.

Another argument against raw is that it is inconvenient and time-consuming, but I think with the development of commercial raw foods, this argument is no longer valid. You can now buy complete commercial raw food, simply thaw it, and feed a single patty.

As I look at the current debate about the raw diet, it does seem like most of the objections relate more to home-cooked diets than raw diets. It's fair to say, I think, that these two approaches are not completely separate. In fact, many home-cooked diets begin with a raw protein base. For example, although I consider myself a "raw feeder" because I rarely cook the dogs' proteins, I am also a "home cook" because I supplement the raw meat with my veggie mix and other add-ons. The ideas I give you for home-cooked meals in this book are based on lightly cooked and steamed foods.

My strategy is a combination of raw protein, home-cooked add-ons, and kibble for Winston. I am fortunate that I have access to a good private supplier of varied proteins that are antibiotic-free, organic, and free-range. I buy my meat once a month. It comes in five-pound "chubs," which I store in the dogs' freezer. When I need one, I defrost it and place it into smaller containers. I weigh out the meal portions, add my veggie mix, and add the various supplements. For Winston, I include a little ground kibble for texture. I'll be the first to admit that this approach is time-intensive and not for everyone. It fits my lifestyle for the moment, but if it doesn't fit yours, you can come up with something that does.

How do I know that what I am adding in is sufficient for each dog's needs? The only result that matters is health! I do my research, make my choices, and I try little changes here and there to see what works. I'll read about the health benefits of chia seeds, for example, and then add it to the veggie mix. The same goes for various greens or flaxseed oil. It's all about being aware of established and emerging information, noting what others are doing, and seeing what works for you. Do I add foods my dogs may not need? Quite possibly. Do I add foods that are dangerous? Absolutely not. This is *food* I'm working with, not *petrochemicals*. The known potentially dangerous foods – avocado, chocolate, grapes/raisins, macadamia nuts, and onions – I stay away from. I check everything I add to be sure it's not potentially toxic for dogs. I have found resources upon which I can depend, and you will also find yours.

Variety is a key to success. Any meal may be lacking in a particular nutrient, but over time, you can ensure your dog receives all the nutrients she needs through the thoughtful use of various foods. If you choose to home-cook, you may start with a canine nutritionist consultation to boost your confidence. If you choose to start on your own, begin by incorporating some kibble to be sure your dog's nutritional needs are being met while you experiment with your own recipes. You can build up slowly as your experience and confidence increase.

Because the dog food world sounds so complex, I think it makes feeding your dog seem more complicated and scarier than it really needs to be. A lot of this is common sense, so take your time. Do some research. Try some new foods. Experiment with recipes. Talk to people about what they're doing. We can all absolutely find our way through this. As we think about improved diets for ourselves, it is a logical next step to improve diets for our dogs. Feeding them well should be no more overwhelming than it is to feed ourselves well.

If you are coming to this book because your dog is fighting cancer, you may receive information from your oncologist that raw proteins are dangerous because of the risk of salmonella and other infections. (There are studies out there about dogs and salmonella, and for many, this is a non-issue. You can read these studies for yourself and come to your own conclusions.) Hear this for what it is: your dog has an impaired immune system due to the cancer and the cancer treatment, and he may not be able to fight off infections well. It is good advice to be cautious, but there are many environmental toxins that present a greater risk to your dog than a commercially prepared raw diet. Bella was raw-fed for her entire chemo treatment, and she did very well. Carefully chosen and clean food can never be a risk to a dog fighting cancer. After researching this topic, you may decide that a commercial raw diet is better for your dog than kibble for rebuilding and supporting an impaired immune system. You may choose to lightly cook your proteins during this period, or you may choose to feed freeze-dried raw. There are many options, but what is crucial is supporting your dog from the inside out, which will include environmental as well as food changes.

How Much to Feed?

The short answer is, not as much as you might think.

This is because when you feed raw or a thoughtful home-cooked diet, you use more whole foods and fewer carbohydrate fillers, so your dog doesn't need as much food to get the necessary nutrients. Right now, your dog may be downing two cups of kibble per meal because the package says that's how much kibble it takes to get the necessary nutrients for that dog's body weight. You can easily accomplish the same nutritional balance with less food if you home-cook or feed a raw diet.

We're all friends here, so let's be honest with one another: the obesity epidemic in the U.S. isn't limited to people. Many of our dogs are pretty portly, too, which is due to the usual culprits – too many calories and too little exercise.

Corgis, for instance, are notorious for packing on the pounds as they live fully by the credo "no crumb too small." For a short-legged, long-backed dog, this is really bad. Both Bella and Winston are normal-sized corgis between 19 and 21 pounds. They have different issues that impact the amount of food they get. Because of Winston's jaw impairment, it takes some work to maintain his 20 pounds. In order for Winston to eat, he has to be muzzled, so his tongue has some support while it scoops food into his mouth. It's a lot of work for him, and he gets tired. When he gets tired, he stops eating and walks away. Winston's food has to be jam-packed with calories so that he can get enough before he tires from eating.

Bella presents a different issue: at 10 she doesn't exercise like she used to, so it's difficult to keep her from gaining weight. Additionally, I add so many herbal supplements to her food that I have to make sure there's enough flavor to keep her eating. I don't want her to get turned off from her meals but that extra flavor can't add too many extra calories. Bella and Winston eat many of the same foods, but they eat them in different amounts.

My friend Jean talks about three levels of weight – athletic weight, normal healthy weight, and overweight, and I think that's a fair way to look at it. If your dog participates in a sport, or if you love to go hiking or swimming with your dog every weekend, you're going to want to keep that dog at an athletic weight, which is slimmer than a normal healthy weight. You can feel some ribs, but the backbone and hips aren't prominent, and the dog carries a lot of muscle. The dog isn't bony, she's athletic. My young Fern is presently at an athletic weight because she chases her ball and moves non-stop all day long. This will change as she ages and once she's spayed. In another few years, I expect her to fill out and mature. We have to recognize that as our dogs' lives change, so do their nutritional requirements.

A normal healthy weight for a non-athlete is just that: you can feel some ribs, you can see a waistline, the dog doesn't pant heavily at normal exertion, and there aren't blobs of fat gathering at the waist. Bella is at a normal healthy weight. She has a clear waistline, but she is not fur-covered muscle like Fern. In both the athlete and the normal-healthy-weight dog, you'll see balance in the way the dog carries herself, regardless of the breed. You'll see a tireless trot. She feels good, she's full of energy, and she doesn't have to work to move around. When I walk my dogs, all three of them move lightly and easily on their leads.

The overweight dog is a different story. We've all seen a heavy, lethargic, panting overweight dog with stiff legs and a dull coat. Allowing a dog to fall into such a state is not healthy, and it's not fair to the dog. They're not fluffy, they're not big-boned – they're fat. These animals may love to eat, but they have no way to regulate their eating, and they depend upon their guardians to do it for them. They may have grown obese on a carb-heavy diet, or they may have medical conditions interfering with how their bodies process food. Regardless of medical conditions, you won't see an obese dog who is raw-fed or on a thoughtfully conceived home-cooked diet.

When researching this book, I looked into how much kibble I should feed Bella, and the information I got was all over the place. One site told me to feed her between 3/4 cup and 1 ½ cups per day. This would be 6-to-12 ounces, which is a useless range of food – this much or twice as much. A second site said she should get between 1 ¼ cups and 1 ¾ cups per day, which works out to 10-to-14 ounces daily. A dog food calculator came in at the surprisingly specific amount of 1.36 cups daily, which is around 11 ounces.

To put it in perspective, Bella gets daily about six ounces of meat and two ounces of add-ins (like veggie mix, kefir, yogurt, eggs, or sardines). This comes to about eight ounces of food daily, as opposed to the kibble range of 6-to-14 ounces daily. As you can see, one difference between kibble and home-cooked or raw is that you use less. Bella's eight ounces of food are packed with nutrients that are easily available to her system, and there are no fillers that her digestive system has to sort through to find the nutrients.

Think about this: we feed more kibble because the dog's digestive system has to sort through a lot of "stuff" to get to the nutrition. Raw diets and home-cooked diets lack that extraneous "stuff," so you feed less. It's the same amount of nutrition but less food.

When you move to a raw or home-cooked meal for your dog, start at a smaller portion and then increase only if you need to. Remember, there's more nutrition in eight ounces of raw food or one cup of home-cooked food than in one cup of kibble, so you can use less of the raw or home-cooked food. This might be hard for you, especially if you've become accustomed to pouring out robust bowls of kibble. It's not going to look like a lot of food, and you'll have to remind yourself that you are feeding a higher quality of food with denser nutrients that will be more available to your dog's digestive system, so she doesn't need as much. You know your dog best, so you'll know if she's dropping weight or losing energy. Just keep an eye on your dog's behavior and readjust as needed. Additionally, take into account changing circumstances. For example, Bella receives three ounces of meat twice daily, but when she and I are on vacation and she's running on the beach several times daily, I bump up her food to about 3.7 ounces twice daily.

Where do treats fit into all this?

Dogs love their cookies. We use treats for fun or for training, but too much of the wrong treats can derail a carefully constructed feeding plan. You need to be as thoughtful with your treats as you are with your food choices. Otherwise, it's like trying to diet while someone is flinging potato chips at you. It can't be done.

Many dogs are over-treated – they have us pretty well-trained when it comes to opening the cookie jar. It's important to remember that dogs don't love us because we treat them. We use treats to reinforce positive behaviors or to train certain behaviors, but we don't use them to buy love. Bella and Fern receive a duck foot at bedtime, and they get treats to reinforce their recalls and support their agility and canine scent-work training, but that's it. And if they've received a lot of training treats (scent work, for example, relies heavily on treating to build a response), I may slightly reduce their protein that day. They don't expect treats at any other time, and it creates confusion when I offer a treat for no reason. Poor Winston doesn't get treated at all because he can't chew, but he loves me all the same.

There are some great treats on the market now, and I've added one of our favorites homemade treats to the recipes section. Think about why and when you want to use treats, and you'll have much more success helping your dog maintain a healthy weight. You'll also feel less manipulated by those big, needy, pleading doggie eyes.

YOU Are the Most Important Ingredient of All

My friend Margaret suggested I add this chapter, and I not only agree with her, I think this may be the most important chapter in the book.

How we look at life, how we perceive what happens in life, and how we put language to occurrences and actions in our lives is incredibly important. As a society, we tend to be pretty negative in our language and perceptions. Wherever you look, the sky seems to be falling.

When we learn that our beloved dog is diagnosed with cancer, our stomachs become sick. We cry. We panic. We question. And we desperately reach out for some kind of rescue, believing a death sentence has been set upon our beloved pet. It does feel like that, I know. Even this year, I lay in bed at night thinking, "Why? Why did she go out of remission? What did I do wrong?"

It's only human to react this way, and it is hard for us to accept that nothing really has changed with our dog. Now, we just have different information about her. How we choose to deal with that information can make a huge difference in the quality of our dog's life, however long that may be. As it could be weeks, months, or years, all any of us truly have are the moments we are in right now.

I have been through this diagnosis twice now with Bella, and you'll still catch me using the language of "fighting the cancer." But that's not really what I'm doing. My job – my only job – is to support Bella's wellness. I give her good food, I protect her from environmental toxins, and I make the best decisions I can in the moment with the information that is available to me.

If you asked me if I meditate, I would say absolutely not; I don't have time. But, actually, I meditate twice a day. For about 10-to-15 minutes, I meditate on the preparation of my dogs' meals. Each meal is a gift of wellness from me to them, tailored to their individual nutritional and physical needs as I understand them. My preparation, as I move from refrigerator to countertop to pantry to shelves of supplements, is like a dance, each motion choreographed with positive feelings and love toward my companions. When I prepare their food, nothing is more important to me. I am focused, and I am enjoying the process whether it's weighing out meat, mincing fresh vegetables, opening supplement capsules, or spooning in yogurt or veggie mix.

I admire their food, and I find their completed meals attractive. I post pictures of them on Bella's social media sites because I take pride in these creations of love. To me, it is my artwork. You would never see a picture of kibbles in a bowl on our pages with the comment, "Look how round and uniform these extruded pellets are!" But I will post and admire the colors and textures of these meals I prepare with my hands infused with feelings of love and goodwill for my dogs. I provide and create healthy meals for my dogs with a sense of gratitude and thankfulness.

And that is a meditation.

This is what I hope for, for you and your dog. As you begin to read these recipes, I want you to feel excitement knowing you are beginning on a path that will bring you closer to your dog while maximizing her level of wellness. Unleash your creativity and trust yourself to use these recipes as a base for good foods that you, yourself, will prepare for your dog.

Thank you for reading this book. It has been my pleasure to write it, and I hope it has brought you enjoyment and energy. Now, on to the fun stuff! Have a great time with the recipes. Don't worry too much about measurements, and tweak them to your heart's content.

Recipes

You can find many books, online forums, and Instagram pages with home-cooking recipes for your dog. The recipes I've included herein I created myself for my dogs' particular nutritional needs. They are basic outlines you can take and tweak to work for your dog's unique circumstances, too. For example, if your dog has a thyroid issue, you may decide to up the iodine content of her food by adding kelp or oysters to your daily veggie mix. If your older dog has dementia, you may choose to increase her daily dose of oily fish or add some algae to support brain functioning. Information about foods and supplements to support specific ailments is easy to access. Talk to your vet, find a holistic vet, join some online forums, and read, read, read.

For the intrepid home cook, there is an infinite variety of meals you can prepare for your dog. Over time and with variation, you can meet all your dog's nutritional needs. However, this is a commitment – you can't rely on a single go-to meal day after day. Variety is key! Perhaps you can home-cook creative meals on weekends, even if your busy weekdays are better suited for a single protein plus supplements or kibble with veggie mix. When I home-cook, I use my veggie mix as an add-on to ensure I'm meeting lots of nutritional high notes.

Home Cooking Basics

Here are some ideas for meals. You might enjoy many combinations yourself, so keep in mind that the meal you are cooking for your dog might also work for you. Unless otherwise noted, all proteins are cooked, and veggies are either lightly cooked or finely chopped to break down the cellular walls for improved digestibility. Remember, your dog's GIT is much shorter than yours, so it can't effectively digest large chunks of raw vegetables. I like to use pickled ginger (what we use for sushi!) for added fermentation and a light drizzle of flaxseed oil for each meal.

- Shredded dark meat chicken, broccoli, sauerkraut, and chicken liver
- Ground beef or buffalo, steamed cauliflower, zucchini, and peas
- Chicken breast, kale, and green bell peppers
- Canned or cooked salmon with skin if available, minced kale, and carrot greens
- Ground beef, steamed beets, and minced kale
- Shredded dark meat chicken, bell peppers, and coconut milk
- Chicken breast, sauerkraut, and broccolini
- Shredded duck, cauliflower, and beets
- Sardines with skin and bone, steamed broccoli, and bone broth

An egg with its shell is a perfect whole food. If you have access to organic eggs that have not been washed or refrigerated, your dog will enjoy the whole egg. Once refrigerated, the shell becomes brittle, and the sharp pieces can poke the gums. Our eggs sit on the counter because they haven't been washed, so the protective film that keeps out bacteria is intact. Add some finely minced veggies.

My two foundational recipes are bone broth and veggie mix, so let's start there. I'm purposefully not providing a lot of measurements, so you can make your own choices as to amounts.

Bone Broth

Bone broth is a super immunity-booster chock full of amino acids. I use it monthly for the dogs unless one is unwell for some reason, in which case I make it a main addition to every meal. It's great for reducing gut inflammation or supporting a move from a grain-based diet to a grain-free diet. It's also good for puppies because the vitamins and minerals build strong bones and muscles, and it helps slim down the obese dog. You can find many recipes online and whole books devoted to bone broth. Here's mine.

What you'll need:
Dutch oven on the stovetop or crockpot

Ingredients:
- Bones with a lot of cartilage (poultry feet, necks, wings, and thighs).
- Distilled water
- Organic apple cider vinegar
- Himalayan pink salt (optional)

Preparation:
1. Place the bones into your pot, and cover with distilled water. Add at least two tablespoons of organic apple cider vinegar. If you have Himalayan pink salt (*not* white table salt), a nice grind will add some extra minerals to your broth, and if you plan on sharing the broth with your dog, you might appreciate a little salt.
2. Bring to a boil and skim the surface scum off several times. Then, turn to low. (If you're using a crock pot, transfer your bones and liquid into it now.)
3. Cook on low for six-to-eight hours before removing and discarding the bones.
4. Chill for several hours. If there's any fat on the top, discard it. Now, you should have a nice jelly. If not, don't worry. Your dog will still love it. Next time, try adding a little more vinegar or a few more feet.

REMEMBER: No cooked bones for your dog, ever! Cooking makes bones brittle, and once broken, the bone slivers can puncture the gut.

Bella's Veggie Mix

As we discussed earlier, a raw diet needs additional veggies, oils, and vitamins. You can put whatever you want into your mix, but be sure to chop or lightly steam your vegetables, so they are more easily digested by your dog and you don't break your blender. Regularly vary your vegetables depending on what is local and in season. Don't use just one veggie; use three or four at least each time, so no two batches are ever the same. Use organic where you can.

What you'll need:
Blender or food processor

Ingredients:

- Fish base (One can of sardines w/bone and skin and packed in water, a half-can of mackerel, plain canned oysters, or plain canned mussels)
- 1 whole organic egg with shell
- 1-2 Tbsp. flaxseed oil
- 1-2 Tsp. coconut oil
- 1 ounce chia seed
- ¼ Cup organic apple cider vinegar
- 1 Tbsp. turmeric (or 1-inch chunk raw, chopped)
- 1 Tsp. ground black pepper
- ¼ Cup pumpkin seeds
- 1 Clove garlic
- 1 Tsp. cinnamon (I add this only in the winter – it's a warming spice)
- 1-inch chunk raw ginger, chopped
- Enough liquid to blend (organic chicken broth, vegetable broth, bone broth, raw goat's milk, kefir, or kombucha; water for overweight dogs or coconut milk for normal weight and athletic dogs.)
- 1 Cup sauerkraut (halve this if you're mixing with kombucha)
- ½ Cup organic blueberries (frozen is ok)

Lots and lots of veggies – carrot greens, romaine lettuce, broccoli, cauliflower, cabbage, parsley, cilantro, asparagus, kale, spinach, zucchini – let your imagination go wild.

Preparation:
1. Blend all ingredients, adding water as needed so the contents are a little slurpy. It will firm up in the refrigerator.

2. Stand back and admire this beautiful green supplement you've just made for your dog.
3. Feed about one spoonful per meal for a small dog or two if your dog is larger.
4. If your batch is too large for your dog to eat in a few days, freeze some for later.

You can add this blend to your raw diet, home-cooked meal, or kibble. It's a great way to get essential nutrients into your dog and feed less kibble simultaneously because, in this form, the nutrients are more bio-available to the dog's digestive system. You don't need a lot of veggie mix, and it's not a 1:1 ratio with kibble. Experiment with half your usual amount of kibble and one spoon of veggie mix for a week and see what you think.

REMEMBER: Do not use any onions, avocado, garlic scapes, grapes, or raisins, as they can be toxic to dogs.

Congee Rice and Chicken

This is our go-to when someone has an upset tummy and diarrhea. We generally fast for the first day to let the pipeline get empty and quiet, and then I feed congee, a rice porridge served as a side dish in many Asian countries. Basically, it's just rice cooked in a lot of water to form a pudding-like texture. That texture comes when the cellular walls of the rice are completely broken down. Our dogs can't digest rice cooked with a 1:2 rice-to-water ratio, so the old "hamburger and rice" staple for many guardians doesn't actually work that well. If we can see the rice as a rice kernel, it's not ready for the dog's GIT. Add more water. The other benefit of congee rice is that it is full of water, so your dog will have less need to drink, which also helps the system calm down.

What you'll need:
Rice cooker or pot

Ingredients:
- ½ Cup white rice (rinsed thoroughly)
- Water
- Chicken (preferably dark meat for higher fat content and more vitamins)

Stovetop Rice Preparation:
1. Start with two cups of water and ½ cup of rice.
2. Bring the water and rice to a boil, stirring frequently so rice does not stick.
3. Turn down the heat once it boils, cover the pot, and simmer for about 15 minutes.
4. Check rice, and continue to add water, ½ cup at a time, until you can no longer see a rice kernel.

Rice Cooker Preparation:
1. Start with four cups of water and ½ cup of rice.
2. Select the congee setting on your rice cooker. *If your rice cooker doesn't have a congee setting, just turn it, pop open the top every 15 minutes, and stir.
3. Add water, ½ cup at a time as necessary, until you can no longer see a rice kernel.

Chicken Preparation:
1. Boil your dark meat chicken lightly.
2. Start adding it to the congee rice on day three.

Portioning:

Fast on Day One. Feed just the congee rice for Day Two. Add some chicken on Day Three. Continue this diet until the poops are normal looking, and then, slowly start to introduce your dog's normal food. I usually keep a dog on some congee rice and chicken for about five days. It's important to give the GIT a break, which is why there's a fast and then a slow introduction of food.

Once your dog's GIT is stabilized, you need to up the probiotics to replenish that system with good bacteria, which have all been blown out by the diarrhea. Slowly rebuild with an herbal supplement as well as food-based probiotics, which are described in the chapter on probiotics.

NOTE: Use white rice, not brown, so this will be easily assimilated by the gut. I really have to push for organic rice here because it has lower lead levels. All rice has lead, so let's keep it to a minimum. The organic rice isn't that expensive, as a little goes a long way, and it can easily be stored. Get the organic white rice.

Summertime Treats

What you'll need:
Ice cube tray

Ingredients:
- Organic blueberries and peaches or steamed veggies (broccoli, zucchini, spinach, kale)
- Coconut milk

Preparation:
1. Place fruits and vegetables into an ice cube tray.
2. Cover with coconut milk and freeze.

Portioning:
One cube makes a tasty, healthy treat on a hot summer day.

Dog Training Treats

These are grain-free and super easy to make. They can be frozen.

What you'll need:
- Food processor or mixing bowl
- Parchment Paper
- Rolling pin
- Oven

Ingredients:
- 1 Can sardines (without water – someone will be happy to drink that for you!)
- 1 Egg (if you're using a food processor, toss that shell in, too, if it's organic)
- 1 Tablespoon chia seeds
- 1 Cup tapioca flour

Preparation:
1. Preheat oven to 350 degrees.
2. Mix all ingredients together really well.
3. Form into a spongy ball.
4. Put the ball between two pieces of parchment paper, and roll it thin.
5. Discard the top piece of paper, and put the bottom one on a cookie sheet.
6. Bake at 350 for about 15 minutes, depending upon the thickness of your dough.
7. Cut with a pizza cutter while warm.
8. Cool completely and store.

NOTE: You can play with the protein – any ground meat like chicken, turkey, venison, or buffalo will work. You can also add 1-2 teaspoons of ground flax seeds, particularly if your dough is too damp, and you don't want to add more flour.

Resources

There is so much information out there, and it is changing fast. I encourage you to do some reading and also to join some online forums, which are full of great ideas from people just like you, who believe they can feed their dogs better. This is by no means an exhaustive listing. However, these are books and magazines I've read and social networking accounts I work with.

Books & Magazines:

The BARF Diet by Dr. Ian Billinghurst

The Goldsteins Wellness & Longevity Program by Dr. Robert S. Goldstein and Susan J. Goldstein (We use this book a lot as the odd issue, like kennel cough, crops up in our lives. It's a great reference book to have on hand.)

Pointing the Bone at Cancer by Dr. Ian Billinghurst (Great for those of you who really want to dig down to the cellular level to understand what happens in cancer.)

Dog Cancer: The Holistic Answer, A Step by Step Guide by Dr. Steven Eisen (This little book got me started on my journey and gave me great hope.)

Henry's Amazing Dog Cancer Diet by Buck Precht

Help Your Dog Fight Cancer, Empowerment for Dog Owners by Laurie Kaplan (One of the first books I read after Bella's diagnosis, which gave me hope that we could find our way through this.)

Dogs Naturally Magazine (There's great information buried deep in this quarterly magazine, and it's a comprehensive resource for finding professionals to support you locally or remotely. The publisher also offers periodic online coursework, which I have found to be tremendously useful.)

Instagram Pages (Great for recipes!):

bella_warrior_princess

whollypets

canine_nutrition

canine_nutritionist

david_caninenutritionist

roorawdoggie

rawfeeding

miamipet.nutrition

rawfeeding

rawfeedingcommunity

truepetdiets

Facebook Pages and Online Forums (More interactive than Instagram, here you'll make helpful connections as you work your way through developing your own diet.):

Bella, Warrior Princess

Canine Nutrition and Natural Health

Best Natural Raw Canine & Feline Nutrition

Rodney Habib Pet Health Site

Healthy Pets with Dr. Karen Becker, presented by Mercola (This site provides daily email updates on nutrition and medical issues for pets.)

The Raw Feeding Community

Prevent Pet Suffocation

About the Author

Jennifer lives in northwest Connecticut on the banks of the Farmington River with her corgis, her collie, her cat, and her chickens. When not working at her small law practice, she is running agility with her dogs or training in canine scent work. She enjoys writing and is currently working on a fiction book about families.

Made in the USA
Lexington, KY
28 February 2018